California Schemin'

by Ron House

A Samuel French Acting Edition

New York Hollywood London Toronto

SAMUELFRENCH.COM

Copyright © 2010 by Ron House

ALL RIGHTS RESERVED

CAUTION: Professionals and amateurs are hereby warned that *CALIFORNIA SCHEMIN'* is subject to a Licensing Fee. It is fully protected under the copyright laws of the United States of America, the British Commonwealth, including Canada, and all other countries of the Copyright Union. All rights, including professional, amateur, motion picture, recitation, lecturing, public reading, radio broadcasting, television and the rights of translation into foreign languages are strictly reserved. In its present form the play is dedicated to the reading public only.

The amateur live stage performance rights to *CALIFORNIA SCHEMIN'* are controlled exclusively by Samuel French, Inc., and licensing arrangements and performance licenses must be secured well in advance of presentation. PLEASE NOTE that amateur royalty fees are set upon application in accordance with your producing circumstances. When applying for a licensing quotation and a performance license please give us the number of performances intended, dates of production, your seating capacity and admission fee. Licensing Fees are payable one week before the opening performance of the play to Samuel French, Inc., at 45 W. 25th Street, New York, NY 10010.

Licensing Fee of the required amount must be paid whether the play is presented for charity or gain and whether or not admission is charged.

Stock licensing fees quoted upon application to Samuel French, Inc.

For all other rights than those stipulated above, apply to: Samuel French, Inc., at 45 W. 25th Street, New York, NY 10010.

Particular emphasis is laid on the question of amateur or professional readings, permission and terms for which must be secured in writing from Samuel French, Inc.

Copying from this book in whole or in part is strictly forbidden by law, and the right of performance is not transferable.

Whenever the play is produced the following notice must appear on all programs, printing and advertising for the play: "Produced by special arrangement with Samuel French, Inc."

Due authorship credit must be given on all programs, printing and advertising for the play.

ISBN 978-0-573-69835-4   Printed in U.S.A.   #29262

No one shall commit or authorize any act or omission by which the copyright of, or the right to copyright, this play may be impaired.

No one shall make any changes in this play for the purpose of production.

Publication of this play does not imply availability for performance. Both amateurs and professionals considering a production are strongly advised in their own interests to apply to Samuel French, Inc., for written permission before starting rehearsals, advertising, or booking a theatre.

No part of this book may be reproduced, stored in a retrieval system, or transmitted in any form, by any means, now known or yet to be invented, including mechanical, electronic, photocopying, recording, videotaping, or otherwise, without the prior written permission of the publisher.

MUSIC USE NOTE

Licensees are solely responsible for obtaining formal written permission from copyright owners to use copyrighted music in the performance of this play and are strongly cautioned to do so. If no such permission is obtained by the licensee, then the licensee must use only original music that the licensee owns and controls. Licensees are solely responsible and liable for all music clearances and shall indemnify the copyright owners of the play and their licensing agent, Samuel French, Inc., against any costs, expenses, losses and liabilities arising from the use of music by licensees.

IMPORTANT BILLING AND CREDIT REQUIREMENTS

All producers of *CALIFORNIA SCHEMIN'* must give credit to the Author of the Play in all programs distributed in connection with performances of the Play, and in all instances in which the title of the Play appears for the purposes of advertising, publicizing or otherwise exploiting the Play and/or a production. The name of the Author *must* appear on a separate line on which no other name appears, immediately following the title and *must* appear in size of type not less than fifty percent of the size of the title type in a legible font.

In addition the following credit *must* be given in all programs and publicity information distributed in association with this piece:

This version of CALIFORNIA SCHEMIN' premiered at Grove Theater Center in Garden Grove, California. Kevin Cochran, Artistic Director. Charles Johanson, Executive Director.

CALIFORNIA SCHEMIN' was first presented on April 18, 1991 at the Florida Studio Theatre in Sarasota, Florida under the original name of *Dynamic Products* (Richard Hopkins, artistic director). The production was directed by Stephen Rothman, with scenic design by Jeffrey W. Dean, sound design by Jon Gottlieb, costume design by Marcella Beckwith & Thomas Preziosi. The cast was as follows:

JULES MERCIER	Bradford Wallace
ROGER GALLAIS	Tony Papenfuss
LOLA MONTEZUMA	Gloria Hayes
NOBBY CARLYSLE	Doug Jones
WANDA HARRINGTON	Julia Flood
SHELLY LEVINE	Lisa Kay Powers
HARVEY MARTIN	Doug Jones

CALIFORNIA SCHEMIN' had its West Coast premiere on January 14, 1997 at the Sacramento Theatre Company in Sacramento, California, (Stephen Rothman, artistic director). The production was directed by Stephen Rothman, with assistant direction by Yawar Charlie, scenic design by Robin Robert, sound design by Jon Gottlieb, costume design by Michael Alan Stein, lighting by Jim Moody, sound design by Gregg Coffin/Brian Noerringer, and choreography by Ron Cisneros. The production stage managers were Betsy M. Martin and Jerry R. Montoya, and the assistant stage manager was Mark Hales. The cast was as follows:

JULES MERCIER	Joe Barnaba
ROGER GALLAIS	Tony Papenfuss
LOLA MONTEZUMA	Elisabeth Nunziato
NOBBY CARLYSLE	Ken Sorkin
WANDA HARRINGTON	Deborah Van Valkenburgh
SHELLY LEVINE	Carrie Dobro
HARVEY MARTIN	Ken Sorkin

CALIFORNIA SCHEMIN' had its Southern Californian premiere on October 27, 1997 at the Grove Theatre Center (Kevin Cochran, artistic director; Charles L. Johanson, executive director), in Garden Grove, California. It was produced in association with Gilbert Adler Productions, Inc. The production was directed by Ron House, with scenic and lighting design by Kevin Cochran, choreography by Francisco Martinez, and costume design by Don Nelson. The production stage manager was Karen Runta The cast was as follows:

JULES MERCIER	Donovan Scott
ROGER GALLAIS	Mark Balnkfield
LOLA MONTEZUMA	Marabina Jaimes
NOBBY CARLYSLE	Oliver Muirhead
WANDA HARRINGTON	Denise Moses
SHELLY LEVINE	Amy Court
HARVEY MARTIN	Oliver Muirhead

CHARACTERS

ROGER GALLAIS - A self-realized genius.
LOLA MONTEZUMA - A former illegal alien.
JULES MERCIER - an inventor of new-age machines.
NOBBY CARLYLE - A fugitive from British justice.
WANDA HARRINGTON - A woman seeking "True Love."
SHELLY LEVINE - A native of New York and would-be comic.
HARVEY MARTIN - A West Hollywood gay activist (same actor as **NOBBY**).

Special thanks to The Audry Kinnis Skirball Foundation,
Los Angeles, California.

ACT I

(Lights up on a cluttered front room of a 1940s West Hollywood bungalow which has been converted into an office. The room has a set of filing cabinets of different heights that can be climbed like a stairs. The transcabator, a new age machine, should be built into the set. There is a TV camera on tripod. There is a photo of **ROGER** *and his wife* **LOLA**. *He wears a white Navy uniform [enlisted man]. She wears a very latin-type dress. The photo is twenty years old.)*

(There are slogan type signs – "TAKE CONTROL OF OTHER PEOPLE'S LIVES," "FIVE WAYS TO RECOGNIZE A REAL LOSER," "A ONE STEP PROGRAM TO SUCCESS," "THE DEFAULT IS NOT MY FAULT.")

(As the lights come up to full, **JULES MERCIER**, *a heavyset man in his fifties, begins to operate a home video camera.)*

*(***ROGER GALLAIS** *enters; he is in his late forties. His taste in clothes is loud and unstylish. He stands in front of transcabator. A TV monitor is somewhere on stage so the audience can see the effect.)*

JULES. Lights! Action!

ROGER. Hello there, you probably recognize me…Yes. I am ROGER GALLAIS, the successful millionaire.

JULES. This is a sixty second commercial!

ROGER. Let me ask you a question. Do you feel that you've been skipped over in life? A lot of people do!

JULES. Forty-five seconds.

ROGER. That's why I invented the TRANSCABATOR. It is a brain-stimulating machine that expands your thought process. Now lets take a typical problem…like, how to pay your ever-mounting bills with your ever-dwindling salary. Use the transcabator

(He sticks his head in the machine. It makes some weird noises.)

Amazing! Astonishing! I never thought of that!

JULES. Thirty seconds!

ROGER. The Trancabator can be yours, for the incredible price of 199.95. That's right, sixteen simple payments of 199.95.

JULES. Nine, eight, seven, six, five,

ROGER. CUT!!!

JULES. Cut! Roger, I don't think we should start selling the transcabator yet?

ROGER. Why not?

JULES. I've only made one and it's a prototype.

ROGER. Jules, you worry too much. It's a gold mine!

JULES. Roger, it's not quite that simple.

ROGER. Life isn't complicated when you understand what to do! And, all you have to do is program my great ideas into this machine

*(**ROGER** picks up a racing form and pays no attention to what **JULES** is saying.)*

JULES. Yes, but it still has to be reprogrammed and I'm not sure…

ROGER. Did you hire a secretary?

JULES. I called "Speedy Temporary Service," but we can't afford to pay her!

*(**JULES** exits.)*

*(The door is flung open and **LOLA MONTEZUMA DE GALLAIS** enters. She is over made up and brassy in her attire. She is very quick-tempered, highly excitable and speaks with a Spanish accent. She carries a large*

envelope stuffed with papers. **ROGER** *hasn't noticed her come in as he is reading the racing form. She hurls the envelope, which strikes him.)*

LOLA. Your eviction notice, Señor Gallais!

ROGER. Look what the cat dragged in! It's my charming and estranged wife, "The Terror of Tijuana"!

LOLA. Haven't you sign the divorce papers, yet?

ROGER. Haven't you been deported yet?

LOLA. This house is mine I own it!

ROGER. I didn't know illegal aliens could own property in California!

LOLA. I'm your wife, so I'm legal! Anyway, this is occupied Mexico! We're throwing the Gringos out! And you're next. *(She points at papers.)*

ROGER. You can't throw me out! I'm a sitting tenant. So you get out, Lola.

LOLA. You better read that, it will tell you how your legal wife – me, Lola Montezuma…

ROGER. Montezuma, isn't that the name of a cheap beer they sell at tourist traps in Tijuana?

LOLA. And isn't Roger Gallais the name of an even cheaper perfume they sell at tourist traps on Hollywood and Vine?

ROGER. Lola, I'm busy!

LOLA. I want you and your super tacky "get rich quick" business out of my house, NOW!

(She begins to throw papers and various things from his desk into the wastepaper basket.)

ROGER. Lola! Stop that!

(JULES enters.)

LOLA. Jules read the eviction notice to the loser.

(JULES picks up the letter.)

JULES. Dear loser…

(ROGER snatches it from him.)

ROGER. *(reading the letter)* Wait a minute, this is against the law.

LOLA. No it isn't! Read the section about the $1500.

JULES. $1500 by 12 o'clock tomorrow or...

ROGER. OR WHAT???

JULES. We are on the street!

ROGER. It only gives me 24 hours! Have a heart!

LOLA. I do, it's made of stone.

JULES. *(reads the letter)* But why are you doing this, Lola?

ROGER. Lola's plan is simple, it has to be, she has a pea-size brain.

LOLA. You have something pea-size too, Roger, and it's not your brain.

ROGER. Very amusing Lola! *(to JULES)* If she gets the sitting tenant out, Me! Then, she and her friend "the fugitive from British justice," will tear down the house and put up a mini mall.

LOLA. That's right and you can't stop us!

ROGER. I hear the "leper from Lime House"...What's his name?

LOLA. Nobby!

ROGER. What a masculine name! That he's wanted in England for, impersonating a human being?

LOLA. I've wasted enough time with you. Fifteen hundred dollars by 12 tomorrow. Speaking of time, it's time you got your junk out of here, and take the masturbator with you.

JULES. It's called a Transcabator.

(LOLA moves toward the backroom.)

ROGER. Hey Lola, you can't go in there, I've got trade secrets in there....

(ROGER and LOLA exit to the office.)

(JULES begins to pick up papers that have been thrown on the floor. He goes under the desk.)

(SFX: Police siren)

(The door is pushed open and **NOBBY CARLYLE** *enters as if he is being chased. He hides and looks out the window. He has a menacing manner.* **NOBBY** *is very paranoid and obviously bothered by the police siren.)*

(emerging from under the desk)

JULES. *(cont.)* Good morning, may I help you?

*(***NOBBY*** gives a start and throws up his hands and leans against the wall in a classic police search stance with legs spread apart. Then realizes* **JULES** *is not the police.)*

NOBBY. I'm looking for Lola.

JULES. She's in a meeting with Mr. Gallais.

(He crosses to the door and opens it. **LOLA** *and* **ROGER** *fall half way out fighting. The door slams.)*

NOBBY. Gawd Blimey, I'll just wait here, then.

JULES. You must be from England…Let me guess…London to be more precise.

NOBBY. *(taking offense)* That's right. What's it to you, then?

JULES. Oh nothing, I was just curious.

NOBBY. Curiosity killed the cat.

*(***JULES*** laughs politely.* **NOBBY** *doesn't.)*

JULES. *Cats.* I saw that in London…*(sings one word)* Memories…I never understood that flying saucer…

NOBBY. I hate musicals!

JULES. It was bad! I hated it too! *(attempting to make polite conversation after a long pause)* We have some great beaches in L.A.

NOBBY. Beaches got crowds. I don't like crowds. You never know who could be in them.

JULES. That's right you never do…ha ha…

*(***NOBBY*** picks up a donut by the coffee pot.)*

Oh, excuse me…but those are for the customers.

*(***NOBBY*** stares angrily at* **JULES** *and then drops the donut back in the box.)*

JULES. *(cont.)* L.A. is the movie capital of the world…What are your favorite movies?

NOBBY. "Lethal Weapon, part one," "Lethal Weapon, part two," "Lethal Weapon, part three," and "The Little Mermaid." *(Note: Actors may use current movie titles.)*

JULES. Interesting choice. What kind of a job did you have in England?

NOBBY. Removals.

JULES. What do you remove?

NOBBY. Who do you want removed?

*(**LOLA** enters with **ROGER**. They are arguing.)*

LOLA. I'll be back at 12 o'clock tomorrow with a wrecking crew.

ROGER. Don't bother!

LOLA. And if you're not out at 12:01, you are going to get wrecked along with the house.

*(She crosses to **NOBBY** and gives him a sexy kiss then stares defiantly at **ROGER** for a moment. She then turns and walks out. **NOBBY** stands grinning at the door. **LOLA** grabs him and pulls him off stage.)*

(There is a moment of stunned silence.)

JULES. Well, it happened again.

ROGER. What?

JULES. What! Every time Lola comes here, she upsets you. I think you're still in love with her, Roger.

ROGER. I'm not in love with her, and I'm not upset. *(Obviously, he is.)*

JULES. Okay…okay…But how can we find the money in twenty four hours? It's impossible!

ROGER. It's not impossible, it's improbable.

*(There is a knock on the door. **ROGER** freezes in terror.)*

(sotto voce) Are you expecting anyone?

*(**JULES** shakes his head.)*

JULES. No!

ROGER. Good!

(There is a loud knock at the door.)

Answer the door!

(He is becoming increasingly paranoid. **JULES** *opens the door.* **ROGER** *hides behind it.)*

JULES. Yes, may I help you?

*(***WANDA HARRINGTON**, *a rather mousy looking woman in her forties, appears at the door. She carries a large suitcase and is very much the "plain Jane" type.)*

WANDA. Good morning, I am looking for Roger Gallais.

*(***ROGER** *slams the door on her suitcase.* **JULES** *kicks the rest of it out.)*

ROGER. Why is she looking for me?

JULES. I don't know…She's probably the secretary from the Temp agency.

ROGER. Secretary ! If you placed the order, why is she asking for me? How does she know my name?

JULES. Err…I don't know!

(They both jump to look out the window.)

She looks like a secretary!

ROGER. Looks are deceiving… *(He laughs in a deranged manner.)* I know who she is…A spy sent by my wife!

JULES. Aren't you being a bit paranoid?

ROGER. No, not paranoid, I am being clever, cunning. Now, let's play them at their own game. Act normal. Pretend you suspect nothing.

JULES. I am acting normal and I don't suspect anything! She's the secretary. I'll send her away.

ROGER. No! Don't you see, that'll prove it!

JULES. Prove what?

ROGER. That we don't have the money.

JULES. We don't have any money, that why I'm sending her away.

ROGER. You're not sending her away! I have a plan to find out what she wants. So, trust me!

(**ROGER** *climbs out the window.* **JULES** *opens the door and* **WANDA** *enters.*)

JULES. Please come in, Miss...

WANDA. Are you Mr. Gallais? The photographer...Gallais photos?

JULES. Oh, you mean Dynamic Photo Dating Service. I am Jules Mercier, the photographer...Please step this way.

(He indicates a chair near the camera tripod.)

WANDA. Thank you.

JULES. Most of our clients have a hot date within a few hours of signing with our dating service.

WANDA. That's nice, but I don't really want a date.

JULES. I see, you're in denial. Don't worry, most clients are, but they're usually married in a year.

WANDA. I'm already engaged.

(He disappears beneath the black camera cloth. **WANDA** *produces an 8x10 black and white picture of a young man and holds it beside her face as* **JULES** *clicks the camera.* **JULES** *sticks his head out from under the cloth.)*

JULES. Excuse me, but what are you doing?

(**ROGER** *enters. He is dressed in the uniform of a "Sparklettes Water" delivery man. He carries a large water bottle that hides his face.*)

ROGER. Good morning, Sparkless Man......

JULES. (**JULES** *does not recognize* **ROGER**.) I'm sorry, we canceled your service months ago. Thank you, we're very busy.

ROGER. Your superior, Roger Gallais reordered the water last week.

WANDA. Roger Gallais! That's why I came here because on this old photo of Henry, that's my fiancé...Look, it says "A Roger Gallais Photo." I thought Roger Gallais might remember him. I didn't really know where to start. I haven't seen Henry in twenty five years. I just arrived in Los Angeles ten minutes ago.

ROGER. I'll just change the bottle like Mr. Gallais ordered.

(**JULES** *grabs the water bottle and they begin to struggle with it.*)

JULES. He hasn't ordered it! I haven't ordered it! She hasn't ordered it. If you don't get out of here, I'll call the police.

ROGER. *(stage whisper)* It's me, you witless worm!

JULES. What!

ROGER. It's me! Gallais! Roger Gallais!

JULES. I didn't know you were working for Sparkless Water!

ROGER. I am not! I am in disguise!

(**JULES**, *realizing his mistake, pulls away from* **ROGER** *as if nothing has happened.*)

JULES. Ah, yes, the water that was ordered last week. It's very nice of you to bring it.

WANDA. When will the picture be ready?

JULES. One hour.

WANDA. Good, I want to find where some acting schools are.

JULES. You want to enroll in an acting school?

WANDA. No, but my fiancé did…Maybe some one at a school would remember him…I guess, you're thinking I'm a little crazy?

(**JULES** *and* **ROGER** *nod their heads in agreement.*)

It's hard for some people to understand how "True Love."

(SFX: Tweeting birds)

It can last your entire life. I fell in love with Henry at the senior prom.

(Romantic music plays.)

WANDA. *(cont.)* He looked into my eyes and said, "May I have the pleasure of this dance?" and I said, "Yes." We danced.

(Wild 70's rock music comes on and she dances to it.)

We were engaged the next day.

JULES. That's a little fast.

WANDA. That's what my Daddy said. He thought Henry wanted to marry me because I was the sole heir to the Harrington oil well millions.

*(**ROGER** reacts when money is mentioned.)*

JULES. Well, what happened?

WANDA. My Daddy has up and died and left me the family fortune. I didn't know what I was going to do with my fortune until I found this in his things…It's from Henry.

(She hands him a post card.)

JULES. *(reading aloud)* Hey Wanda, L.A. is rough, I've run out of bread! Can you send me anything? I'm miming in street theatre at Venice Beach California. But it don't pay too much. *(stops reading)* But it's postmarked 1983! *(a date 20 years before)*

WANDA. Yes, it's "true love."

(SFX. Tweeting birds)

It can last your entire life. Do you think I'm crazy?

ROGER. Of course not! But you'll need a good detective agency. And they can be expensive.

WANDA. Oh, money's no problem…

ROGER. Well, I have to be on my way…More water to deliver and good luck, and yes, and here's the water bill…I made it out to Roger Gallais Detective Agency.

JULES. You what?…We don't have –

ROGER. You know, the ones who specialize in missing persons cases…Well…so long.

(**ROGER** *rushes offstage pushing the water bottles.*)

WANDA. You have an agency that specializes in missing persons?

(**JULES** *stares at her for a long indecisive moment.*)

JULES. Yes, we do…and I hope, that the head of the detective agency will be here soon.

WANDA. May I use the bathroom?

JULES. Sure the key is hanging on the wall. Through that door and on the left.

(**WANDA** *exits.* **ROGER** *enters. He now wears a trench coat and wide brimmed hat.*)

We don't have a detective agency!

ROGER. We do now!

JULES. But I don't understand?

ROGER. Look, there's the money we need. Don't you listen? She just inherited an oil well.

JULES. But we…

ROGER. I have a plan, just play along.

(**WANDA** *enters.* **ROGER** *pretends he doesn't notice her and does an imitation of Humphrey Bogart's Sam Spade.*)

(*SFX: 40s spy movie music*)

Yes, the Graves case was hard. The cops was stumped. But in a couple of days I put the family back together. I'm beat. You know, it's hard to believe but they hadn't seen each other in twenty four years.

(**ROGER** *puts his feet on the desk and slips and falls behind the desk.*)

(*noticing* **WANDA**) Is this our new secretary? Take a letter…

WANDA. I'm Wanda Harrington, but I'm not the new secretary…I'm…I guess, I'm a customer.

ROGER. Oh, I'm real sorry, sweetheart, but we ain't taking no new cases.

WANDA. Oh, please…I'll pay any price.

ROGER. Okay, you look like a swell tomato. I'll make an exception. Who are you looking for?

WANDA. *(producing photograph)* Him!

ROGER. Hmmm…This was taken about twenty five years ago. This is your fiancé!

WANDA. Amazing!…Could you please take the case?

ROGER. Jules, put all my other cases on hold and do a sketch of the missing person.

(JULES takes a phone off the hook and gets a sketch pad.)

Can you describe him for me?

(She begins to describe JULES and what he's doing.)

WANDA. He has a receding hair line, he's about 5'6" and he's sketching on a pad.

(The description should match the actor playing JULES.)

ROGER. No, not him! *(pointing to JULES)* Him! *(points to the photograph)*

WANDA. He was tall but not too tall and he weighted 165 pounds maybe more, jet black hair, a cute little mouth and eyes that twinkled like stars…and let me think…

JULES. Is that him?

WANDA. That's him!

(JULES produces a picture from his sketch pad that looks exactly like the photo that WANDA brought. ROGER is annoyed and grabs the pad from JULES.)

ROGER. He could have changed a lot. Do you think you'd recognize him today?

WANDA. Yes…I think so…Well, I don't know.

ROGER. Well, we're real busy and detective work can set you back a few potatoes.

WANDA. How many?

ROGER. Fifteen hundred clams.

WANDA. Oh, no problem, I'd pay twice that.

(**ROGER** *annoyed that he didn't ask for more.*)

How long will it take to find him?

ROGER. It could take a long time, unless, you ordered a "rush job." That's an extra two thousand smackers.

WANDA. Okay! Then how long would it take?

ROGER. I'll have him here by the time you come back for your pictures.

JULES. But that's in less than an hour!

ROGER. Yes, I know!...Remember, I'm good at my job. *(to* **WANDA***)* So come back in an hour, sweetheart and we'll have him for you.

WANDA. Just think, by this time tomorrow Henry and I could be married. Oh, I'm so excited. I'm going to look at wedding dresses.

(She exits.)

ROGER. *(jumping with joy)* Here comes the bride!

JULES. Roger, are you crazy? How can we find a man that has been missing for 25 years in less than an hour?

ROGER. I have already found him, remember her description?

JULES. Yes, I got it, dark hair, tall but not too tall, medium build...Millions of guys look like that! It could be anyone.

ROGER. You're right, it could be anyone...You could be Henry.

JULES. What!...She's already seen me!

ROGER. She hasn't seen you in disguise.

JULES. You want me to get into a disguise and pretend to be her long-lost lover?

ROGER. Yeah...It's a great idea!

JULES. Okay, I'm in disguise. We talk. In a couple of minutes she's asking me questions about people I never met. What do I say – I don't want to talk?

ROGER. You want to talk but you can't!

JULES. What! Why can't I talk?

ROGER. I don't know.

JULES. So you see, it's not going to work.

ROGER. It's gotta work, we gotta think of something! You can't talk because…You took a vow not to talk.

JULES. Why would I do something like that?

ROGER. Like a priest, he's a priest and he took a vow of silence.

JULES. He was an actor.

ROGER. An actor…no he wasn't an actor. He was a mime. Mimes don't talk, right?

JULES. If they talked they wouldn't be mimes.

*(**ROGER** begins to move his hands like a mime.)*

ROGER. I've got it! He's a mime and he took a vow of silence…Jules, this is a brilliant idea!

JULES. Do mimes take vows of silence?

ROGER. I don't know! AND I DON'T CARE!…Instead of talking to her, you'll mime.

JULES. Come on, Roger! I don't know how to mime!

ROGER. It's easy! That French jerk Marcel Marceau made a million bucks walking against the wind with a balloon.

*(**ROGER** mimes walking in the wind **JULES** follows him.)*

JULES. Okay…if she goes for it she'll want to marry me.

ROGER. You're right and there's only one thing that can prevent that.

JULES. And that is…?

ROGER. DEATH!

JULES. I've given a lot for the company but that's too much…

*(He attacks **ROGER** and begins to strangle him. **ROGER** frees himself and reacts as if nothing has happened.)*

ROGER. I don't mean a real death! We'll fake your death! You'll collapse suddenly and fall into a comma. A doctor will come and pronounce you dead.

JULES. A doctor won't do that. He'd lose his license!

ROGER. It won't be a real doctor.

JULES. Then who will it be?

ROGER. It'll be me disguised as a doctor. I'll pronounce you dead at the scene!

JULES. But you'll be right there. What do you say? – "Excuse me while I go change into my Doctor disguise."

ROGER. I come up with these great ideas and then you just stamp on them with logic!! But you won't get away with it this time! I'll say the phone is out of order! So I'll have to go out and get a doctor and then I come back in disguise…This is a brilliant idea, Jules!

JULES. No! It's dishonest, and I won't do it, Roger! I have integrity! Have you ever heard of principles? NO!!

*(**ROGER** becomes soft and teary)*

ROGER. You're right, Jules. It was wrong of me to ask you. You've got principles. Forget it! Forget about the guy who went broke investing in your machine. The transcabator! Because of you his marriage broke up! Because of you he lost his home! Because of you he's no longer a pet owner!

JULES. You told me to back the car up!

ROGER. I loved that dog.

*(**ROGER** cries and **JULES** follows suit. But **ROGER**'s tears are false, **JULES**' aren't.)*

JULES. Okay, okay, I'll do it, but I don't have to like it… Look, it's almost ten thirty.

ROGER. She'll be back soon. Let's go get the mime stuff and drop her pictures off at Thrifty's.

*(**ROGER** and **JULES** exit.)*

*(A moment passes, **NOBBY** appears at the window; he jimmies it open and climbs in. He opens the door. **LOLA** enters. They begin to search the office.)*

LOLA. I know it gotta be here somewhere!

NOBBY. Yeah, but we need time to find it.

LOLA. We don't have time, Nobby!

NOBBY. There's millions of files here plus the safe! It could be anywhere.

(He finds a file and pulls out some papers.)

Here it is! Bollocks! It's a bloody photocopy!

LOLA. Let me see it !

(He hands her the paper she reads it intensely.)

¡Qué, mala suerte!

NOBBY. WHAT! WHAT!

LOLA. ¡Mil novecientos trentinueve! Maldición…1939!

NOBBY. What?

LOLA. At 12 tomorrow we take possession of the building but…let me see that newspaper…

*(**NOBBY** hands her a newspaper. She reads:)*

"The West Hollywood moratorium on demolition of all buildings constructed before 1940 went into effect today. Gay activist Harvey Martin sponsored the bill."

NOBBY. Gay activist Harvey bloody Martin, I'd like to ring his poncy, homosexual neck.

LOLA. Even if we have possession of the building, the City will stop us from tearing it down right…Unless…

(a long pause)

NOBBY. Unless…what?

LOLA. Unless…you blow up the building.

NOBBY. Hey, you can go to jail for something like that!

LOLA. *(sexily)* Then we'd have to tear it down…and put up a mini mall… *(She starts rubbing her legs on his.)* It would be so easy for you…

*(**NOBBY** reacts to her advances.)*

NOBBY. Come on, love, don't start that.

LOLA. Do it for Lola…And, then Lola will do "it" for you.

*(She kisses him passionately and then moves away. **NOBBY**'s lust begins to rise.)*

NOBBY. Oh, Lola!

(She puts up her hand to stop him from touching her.)

LOLA. No boom, no bang!

*(**NOBBY**, realizing he'll have to obey **LOLA** to get what he wants, begins to examine the room.)*

NOBBY. Hmm…the heater, it looks a bit dodgy. They cause terrible accidents, them heaters.

LOLA. You could make it look like an accident, no?

NOBBY. I was a professional accident arranger in London… Let me see, there must be a pipe under the floor.

LOLA. Eso, Nobby.

NOBBY. Nay, it ain't gonna work.

LOLA. Why not?

NOBBY. Because I'd need time in the basement to rig it… Roger and his mate are goin' be back in a few minutes.

LOLA. I think I've got an idea that'll work.

(SFX: noise of a car wreck)

*(**LOLA** looks out the window and laughs.)*

Roger has just rear ended Mr. Chang from next door.

CHANG. *(off)* You wreck my car! I sue you!

ROGER. *(off)* That's my parking spot!

CHANG. *(off)* Gallais, you loser. I sue. My brother-in-law big man in Korea!

LOLA. Here come the cabrones. Vamonos!

*(They exit. **ROGER** and **JULES** enter carrying some packages. **ROGER** yells out the window.)*

ROGER. I don't care if your bother-in-law is the king of Korea. I don't care if he's Chick Corea!

JULES. Look, it's almost 11 o'clock.

ROGER. She won't be here for another half hour.

(There is a knock at the door.)

She's early…stall her.

(**ROGER** *exits carrying the packages.*)

(**SHELLY LEVINE** *enters. She is rather brassy, and a well developed Jewish girl in her thirties or more. She wears extremely tight sexy clothes. She speaks with a pronounced New York accent.*)

SHELLY. Hi, I'm Shelly from "Speedy Temps." Sorry, I'm late. I'm looking for emeralds..no diamonds...rubies... What is it?...Jules!

JULES. I'm Jules.

SHELLY. Here's my curriculum vitae. *(looking at the surrounds)* What a dump!

JULES. Hi, I'm sorry but there's been a bit of confusion here. We don't need a secretary.

SHELLY. Oh, God, I've schlepped all the way here and now no job! In New York this would never happen.

(**ROGER** *enters.*)

ROGER. Just a minute, Jules, I don't need a secretary, but I do need a personal assistant!

JULES. This is the boss, Roger.

(**ROGER** *stares lustfully at her.*)

ROGER. How do you do, Ms. Levine. *(mispronounces her name)*

SHELLY. Levine. How do you do, Mr. Gallais. *(mispronounces his name)*

ROGER. Gallais. A lot better since I met you. I need someone like you to work under me.

SHELLY. In New York, I worked under some really big guys.

ROGER. I hope I measure up.

SHELLY. Put your best foot forward.

ROGER. Well, maybe not a foot.

(They both laugh.)

JULES. I see, you've just come out from New York?

SHELLY. Yes, but I've been here eight years.

JULES. You've been a secretary here for eight years?

SHELLY. Are you kidding? I'm just filling in here with a temp job before pilot season.

JULES. Pilot season? You work for the airlines?

SHELLY. No, TV pilots. Where did you get this guy? I'm an actress and a stand-up comic. Shelly Levine, haven't you heard of me?

JULES. No.

SHELLY. You're really out of touch!

ROGER. I'd love to touch your ass...See your ass...act.

SHELLY. Yeah, I'll bet you would.

JULES. Excuse me, but shouldn't you go get the pictures? Remember, she'll be here soon.

ROGER. Excuse me, I have an important meeting at Thrifty Drug store. But, I'll be back very soon and you can get to know me a little better.

*(**ROGER** exits.)*

SHELLY. Boy, I haven't seen anybody that horny since I dated Vito Scarletti from Carmine Street.

JULES. Let's talk about the files.

(He points to a bank of filing cabinets. They are arranged like stairs.)

SHELLY. Those are your files?

JULES. Yes, they are.

SHELLY. *(almost laughing)* In New York everybody's files are computerized.

JULES. That's nice but we're in L.A.

(He climbs on top of the filing cabinets.)

Now, supposing you want to look up something like... Dave's Auto Parts.

SHELLY. Oh, that's real hard but let me guess...You'd look under "D"?

JULES. No, under "H." But come up here, I'll show you.

SHELLY. Why are you climbing on top of the file cabinets?

JULES. The springs are broken, so the drawers won't open. Our weight will counter balance...

SHELLY. Whatever, I'm only here for the day.

*(**SHELLY** climbs up with **JULES**' help. His hand slips.)*

Hey, don't get fresh!

JULES. Sorry…Yes "H" *(He stares at her rear.)* "H" for hinny…for horse power.

(He stamps on the cabinet and the drawers shoot open and close.)

SHELLY. My nails…that's thirty-five dollars.

JULES. It would also be crossed reference under "T" *(He stares at her breasts.)* for transmission. *(He thumbs through files.)* Because Dave's auto fixed the transmission on Roger's car. But about a week later the transmission fell on the ground so it filed under "L" for law suit.

SHELLY. I see, that makes sense. This seems like a great job for a mountain goat.

*(The phone rings. **JULES** leaves **SHELLY** stranded about four feet off the ground.)*

JULES. *(to phone)* Good Morning…Sheba…No we don't - Murray Goldstein?

SHELLY. It's for me! It's my agent! Help! Help! I have vertigo! I'm going to fall.

*(**SHELLY** runs up and down the cabinets, which are various heights. The drawers shoot open. **JULES** dodges them. She falls from the filing cabinets and **JULES** carries her to the desk. They are both tangled in the phone cord. **JULES**' head ends up in **SHELLY**'s crotch, she should appear to be tied up by the phone cord as **ROGER** enters **JULES**' head is in **SHELLY**'s crouch with a phone.)*

JULES. I'll put her on hold!

ROGER. Busy as a beaver, are we?

SHELLY. Yes, I'm learning filing.

JULES. She's really good!

ROGER. Jules, we have an important customer coming in a few minutes.

JULES. Well, I'm just a little tied up.

(They exit.)

(SHELLY begins to put on lipstick. NOBBY enters through the window startling her and she puts a line of lipstick across her face. NOBBY is dressed as a gas man and wears a welder's mask. SHELLY holds up a breath freshener as if it were mace.)

SHELLY. I'm trained in how to use this! *(She squirts herself in the face.)*

NOBBY. Gas board…I'm here to fix the heater.

SHELLY. Heater? What do we want a heater fixed for?

LOLA. *(offstage)* They're dangerous and could blow up the house when you turn them on!

NOBBY. What?

SHELLY. She said *(imitating LOLA's Spanish accent)* They're dangerous and could blow up the house when you turn them on!

NOBBY. That's right!

SHELLY. Heater? You might have noticed that it's about 106 degrees. It's August, in Los Angeles California. Why are we going to turn on the heater?

NOBBY. Er…Well, you perhaps…I think…

SHELLY. I think you were beamed down to the wrong planet. Maybe, you were supposed to fix heaters on Mars. This is earth.

NOBBY. Very amusing. I've got me orders.

SHELLY. From where the death star. Darth Vader only you could be so bold.

(SHELLY laughs hysterically at her own joke. NOBBY looks at her.)

It's a joke. Like funny. Okay, I just work here. Go ahead, do your thing.

(NOBBY crosses to the wall heater. He takes off the front and adjusts the pipes.)

NOBBY. Very dodgy these older heater…I have to go into the basement to rig…fix the heater.

(He goes through trap door.)

(beat)

*(**SHELLY** makes a phone call.)*

SHELLY. Hello, is this Sheldon?...I'm Shelly. I saw your ad. *(She reads from L.A. Weekly)* "Ex-New Yorker disgusted with plastic singles in California." *(stops reading)* No, I don't mind answering. I'm Jewish, forty tw-...twenty-two...I'm an actress and comedienne...I'm on tonight at the Comedy Store, "Open Mike." Would you like some seats?...No, you're right, it's too early in our relationship...Lunch? I'd love to! At Spaggo's. Oh, near Spaggo's. How will I know you?...You're a Jewish version of Brad Pitt and Antonio Banderas? You're a doctor at Cedar Sinai! You'll pick me up in your black BMW.

*(**SHELLY** hangs up.)*

SHELLY. *(cont.)* It couldn't be more perfect. A Jewish Doctor version of Antonio Banderas and Brad Pit. *(current popular leading men)* What will I wear!

(A knock at the door.)

He's early! I'm not ready!

*(**WANDA** enters as **SHELLY** moves toward the door. They collide.)*

WANDA. Is Roger Gallais here?

SHELLY. He died, didn't he?

WANDA. Roger Gallais died?

SHELLY. Oh, I thought you said Robert Goulette, I loved him! Look, could you do me a favor?

WANDA. Well, I don't know...What is it?

SHELLY. There's a very important person is coming. He's a Jewish Doctor version of Antonio Banderas and Brad Pitt! I'm dressing. Tell him to wait!

*(**SHELLY** exits and **ROGER** enters in his detective outfit.)*

WANDA. Well? Did you find him?

ROGER. Yeah, I got him, alright, but it wasn't easy. He's changed a lot. Maybe you won't recognize him.

WANDA. Don't worry, I'd know Henry anywhere. Oh, thank you Mr. Gallais…I can't wait! Where is he?

ROGER. In there, I'll go get him.

*(**ROGER** exits for a moment and then reenters carrying **JULES** like a mannequin. He is in white face and wears a hat with a flower. He stands motionless.)*

WANDA. Henry…I can't believe it's really you…You've changed so much. I hardly recognize you…Why do you have that white stuff on your face? *(He mimes.)* What's he doing?

ROGER. Oh, I forgot to tell you. Henry's a mime.

WANDA. Why don't you say something?

ROGER. He's taken a vow of silence.

WANDA. What? I've never heard of such a thing. How does he communicate?

ROGER. He mimes everything…Ah, mime a feeling for us…Henry…*(**JULES** mimes everything that **ROGER** says.)* You see, he's sad…Now, he's happy…because he has a balloon…Now he's walking against the wind.

WANDA. Look, I don't want to see him mime! I want to know if our love endured?

ROGER. Sure you do. Henry, mime how you feel about Wanda. Oops, it's too late. He's mimed himself into a box.

*(After **JULES** mimes being stuck inside a box, he goes into his motionless state.)*

Oh, did you bring the cheque?

WANDA. Oh, yes, of course. *(She searches in her bag and hands him a cheque.)*

ROGER. It's too bad we can't join him in his mime world. Life is so short.

*(**ROGER** pushes **WANDA** out the door. He breathes a sigh of relief. **WANDA**, suddenly, enters through the window.)*

WANDA. I've got an idea how I can join him in his mime world.

ROGER. How?

(WANDA mimes opening a door and pulls JULES from his mime box. He is delighted, he picks a flower for her. They skip and play like children. ROGER finds all of this exasperating and begins to mime various deaths behind WANDA's back – they fly a kite together. ROGER grabs a real scissors from the desk and cuts the mime string of the kite. JULES falls dead.)

WANDA. Oh, My God! He's fallen and can't get up.

ROGER. I'll go out and get a doctor.

WANDA. Use the telephone!

ROGER. I can't, it's out of order!

(The phone rings.)

WANDA. No it isn't!

(ROGER pulls the phone from its socket.)

ROGER. Oh, that was from next door. Anyway, this is a pencil sharpener! It just looks like a phone! I'd better go and get a doctor.

WANDA. But the line just came out of the jack...Put it back in.

(He exits.)

(bursting into tears) Oh, my darling, I've just found you! Don't leave me...Oh, please don't...

(She rushes to him, giving him several hard CPR type heart blow. He jumps up.)

You're alright?

JULES. I'm fine!

WANDA. You can talk?...Oh, Henry, I've waited so long for this moment, it's wonderful!

JULES. Look, I can't go through with this.

WANDA. You don't love me? Don't you remember the promise you made on prom night?

JULES. No, I don't remember.

WANDA. Oh no…Don't tell me you have amnesia, I see… I wasn't expecting this…but it does explain why you didn't write.

JULES. I don't have amnesia and I'm not Henry! Let me explain, I came to L.A. a long time ago…

WANDA. How long ago?

JULES. I don't even remember!

WANDA. You see, you have amnesia!

JULES. NO, I DON'T!

WANDA. Then, why did you become a mime? Are you a missing person?

JULES. Will you forget about mimes and missing persons for just a minute and listen. This is a con…but I can't con you. It's just not right.

WANDA. You're very nice for a con man.

JULES. What?

WANDA. *(louder)* I said, you're very nice for a con man.

JULES. Yeah, that's what I thought you said. Now, you'd better get out of here before Roger comes back.

(They look at each other for a long moment and are about to kiss, but suddenly, an arriving car breaks the spell.)

It's the doctor. I mean, it's Roger's doctor…Mr. Roger.. He's in the neighborhood.

WANDA. I don't understand, Roger and a Doctor…

JULES. You've got to get out of here.

WANDA. But, I don't want to! I've just found you.

JULES. I'm not who you think I am! Now, here's your cheque. Go on before it's too late.

*(***JULES*** lays on the floor.)*

WANDA. What are you doing?

JULES. I'm going to die!

WANDA. Oh, no!

(She rushes to **JULES** *and starts to heart punch him again.)*

JULES. I'm pretending to die. I'll just say to Roger that you left. Okay?

WANDA. If you say so, okay.

(There is a lover's moment. Then she exits.)

*(***LOLA*** enters from the window. She steps on filing cabinets. A drawer shoots out and hits* **JULES**, *knocking him unconscious.* **LOLA** *does not notice* **JULES** *on the floor. She sees the open trap door and crosses to it.)*

LOLA. Nobby! Nobby! Are you down there?

(No response. She throws a heavy object down the hole [hammer].)

NOBBY. *(coming out of the hole)* There, I've done it! It's rigged.

LOLA. Great, how does it work?

NOBBY. It's simple, but first I have to rig the heater valve.

(He goes over to the heater and turns some knobs and attaches a wire. He bends over with rear sticking out.)

LOLA. Nobby, I smell gas.

NOBBY. A little always escapes when you're working… *(pointing)* That's the switch.

LOLA. *(reaching for the switch)* Do you turn it?

NOBBY. *(knocking her hand away)* NO! Don't turn it! You'll blow up the place!

LOLA. *(admiringly)* Oh, Nobby, you just saved my life.

NOBBY. Yeah, I suppose I did, but it was nothing, really, love.

LOLA. I think you're the smartest guy I've ever had and definitely the best lover. You really know how to turn me on.

(They embrace in a very sexy kiss. He picks her up and puts her on the desk she wraps her legs around him. Then suddenly he sees **JULES** *lying on the floor.)*

NOBBY. Jesus Christ!

LOLA. *(disappointed)* That was quick!

NOBBY. Bleeding hell! Look at 'im ! He's dead! It was probably the gas.

LOLA. Are you sure he's dead?

NOBBY. Just look at his face. He's as white as a sheet!

(Dog barks, they both freeze.)

Someone's coming!

LOLA. Wrap him in the rug and put him in the closet…like a human burrito.

*(He wraps **JULES** in a rug and puts him in the closet.)*

You've killed him!

NOBBY. Me! This was your idea!

LOLA. Yeah, but you let the gas escape into the house! I thought you knew what you were doing.

NOBBY. I do know what I am doing.

LOLA. So do I and it's called murder! I don't know what I saw in you in the first place!

NOBBY. I don't know how I could be so stupid to get mixed up with a Tijuana tart like you.

LOLA. You're a loser, Nobby.

NOBBY. I suppose I'm lucky that I haven't caught any venereal diseases!

LOLA. Shut up! We gotta think of something!…Nobody's here! If we blow the place up right now, the body will be destroyed in the fire.

NOBBY. Good idea! Destroy the body in the fire.

LOLA. How does this thing work?

NOBBY. Quite simple. You turn that switch. It'll take about two minutes.

LOLA. So once that's turned on, you've got two minutes before the house blows up?…Right?

NOBBY. Right!…That is more or less.

LOLA. Well, which is it? More or less?

NOBBY. Give or take a minute.

LOLA. Are you sure this is going to work?

NOBBY. Of course, it will!...I think.

LOLA. Have you taken stupid pills this morning?

NOBBY. No, I don't need them!

LOLA. No, I guess you don't. *(noises off)*. Someone's coming.

NOBBY. Go on, get out the back!

LOLA. What about you?

NOBBY. I'm the gas man. I'm suppose to be here. Isn't I?

*(She exits. A beat and **ROGER** enters wearing his doctor's disguise. He has a black wig, thick glasses and speaks with an nondescript Middle Eastern accent.)*

ROGER. I hope I am not too late. *(sees **NOBBY**)* Who are you?

NOBBY. I'm the gas man. Who are you?

ROGER. I am Doctor Kumars Bacshandi from Cedar Sinai medical hospital. Where's the dead man?

NOBBY. DEAD Man! There's no dead man around here! So, if I was you Governor, I'd clear out before the house blows up!

*(**NOBBY** pushes him out the door a beat and **ROGER** returns.)*

ROGER. Blow up? Why is the house going to blow up?

NOBBY. It isn't! I mean, it couldn't...I just rigged...fixed the heater. The heater is very dodgy. I'm fixing it.

*(**SHELLY** enters. She is overdressed and overdone. Romantic music can be heard.)*

Did you call a doctor?

SHELLY. Yes, is he here?

*(**SHELLY** moves around the stage rhythmically to the music. She is trying to be very sexy but bangs into things and generally causes a mess.)*

ROGER. I am the doctor you called.

SHELLY. Hi, I'm Shelly Levine, I'm so pleased to meet you.

ROGER. I am also pleased to meet you...I want your body!

SHELLY. I beg your pardon!

ROGER. I am coming…

SHELLY. You're coming and you want my body?

ROGER. Yes! I am coming for your body!

SHELLY. What kind of a pervert are you? We haven't even had lunch.

ROGER. Lunch! I don't want lunch! I just want your body.

SHELLY. I don't know what kind of a girl you think I am…

ROGER. I am sure you are a nice girl.

SHELLY. You're not a Jewish doctor version of Brad Pitt and Antonio Banderas. You look more like an ad for The Hair Club for Men. And you don't sound like you're from New York!

ROGER. No, I am from Tehran Iran. There must be a body, otherwise the hospital wouldn't have sent me. *(He starts to look around.)* You can never tell, it might be anywhere.

(He heads toward the closet. **NOBBY** *jumps in front of the door.)*

NOBBY. You can't go in there.

ROGER. Why not?

NOBBY. The heater's in there and I'm working on it.

ROGER. If the heater is in the closet, then what's that? *(He indicates the heater.)*

NOBBY. That's the heater I'm putting in the closet.

SHELLY. Here on earth, we don't put heaters in closets. And we don't fix them in the middle of a heat wave.

*(***NOBBY*** climbs on the file cabinets.)*

NOBBY. That's right, it's not fixed yet…Isn't that Pamela Anderson? *(Note: Actor may substitute name of current scandalous star.)*

(They look as he ducks out the window.)

SHELLY. Pamy, did he hurt you?

*(***ROGER*** opens the closet door and the rug falls out with* **JULES** *in it.* **SHELLY** *screams.)*

How did he get in there? Who's that?

ROGER. *(examining* **JULES***)* Oh, Tandoori chicken! It doesn't look good. He has no pulse.

SHELLY. I've never seen anyone with skin so white!

ROGER. Oh, no, I'm going to have some terrible news for the young lady when she arrives.

*(***WANDA*** enters and sees* **JULES** *on the floor.)*

I'm afraid I have some terrible news for you, Mrs. Wanda.

WANDA. I know, he has amnesia.

ROGER. He has…what?

SHELLY. You know him?

WANDA. *(whispering)* Yes, he has amnesia…He says he's not Henry!

ROGER. I thought he couldn't talk. I thought he was a mime and took a vow of silence.

SHELLY. Do mimes do take a vow of silence?

ROGER. I DON'T KNOW! AND I DON'T CARE! Sorry…

WANDA. The sweet darling is trying to protect me. He says, Roger Gallais is a con man! Look, he gave me my cheque back. *(She places cheque on the desk.)* He's pretending to be dead.

ROGER. How wonderful that he's not dead…but, since he's not dead and I am here, I will give him rectal examination.

(He unrolls **JULES** *from the rug and pushes him toward the desk.* **JULES** *hits the desk and leans over as if to receive a rectal examination.* **ROGER** *put on a rubber glove and* **JULES** *reacts by sitting on the desk.)*

(He begins to examine him very roughly.)

Now, does it hurt when I do this?

(He punches **JULES** *in the stomach.)*

JULES. Yes…

ROGER. Good, that's a normal reaction. Let me test your reflexes. Does this hurt?

(He stamps on **JULES** *feet.)*

JULES. Not as much as when you did this!

(He punches **ROGER** *in the stomach.)*

WANDA. Isn't he a little rough for a doctor?

SHELLY. He's exactly like my gynecologist in Flatbush.

(He takes a regular doctor's hammer out of his bag and then throws it away. He takes a big hammer off the wall. He swings at **JULES**' *knee with a hammer.* **JULES** *jumps out of the way.* **ROGER** *begins to stalk him.)*

ROGER. So the only thing wrong with you is amnesia? Do you remember how you got it?

JULES. No…

SHELLY. Did you fall and hit your head?

WANDA. Were you in some kind of an accident?

JULES. Not that I remember.

ROGER. But then you wouldn't remember…because you have amnesia…A blow to the head can cause amnesia but sometimes, another blow to the head can cure amnesia.

*(***ROGER*** takes a wild swing at* **JULES** *who ducks and he connects with alarm, which goes off.)*

*(***JULES*** exits.)*

Oh, my hand! Oh my God, my hand! I've cut my hand!

WANDA. Oh, Blood! Blood! Blood! I can't stand blood! I feel faint. Where's the bathroom?

SHELLY. Take the key on the wall. It's through that door. Here, honey, I'll help you!

*(***WANDA*** takes the key and unsteadily makes her way to the bathroom led by* **SHELLY**. *She leaves her cheque on the desk.)*

ROGER. Bells, I can't stand the sound of bells.

(He punches the alarm with his good hand and reacts to the pain. The alarm stops.)

(He opens the window and the alarm goes off. He slams the window shut. It swings back and hits him in the face.)

(JULES *enters with a towel wiping his face. He is back in his regular costume. He places the towel on the desk, which is preset with clown white.*)

(hold his hand) Now look what you made me do!

JULES. Me! I haven't done anything!

ROGER. Why did you tell her I was a con man? Why did you give her the cheque back?

JULES. Why? Because you are a con man and I've got a conscience.

ROGER. We gotta to pay the rent or we'll be on the streets. I can't live on the streets! I don't know how to control the shopping carts! I'm allergic to cardboard!

JULES. She's a poor innocent kid…Well, she's not a kid anymore but you know what I mean.

ROGER. Yeah, now hear what I mean! She is going to give us the money and that will solve our problem! So, I'm going to the bank with this cheque before it's too late.

BOTH. The CHEQUE!

(JULES *grabs the cheque. They wrestle over it.* **WANDA** *enters with* **SHELLY**.)

SHELLY. Are you alright now?

WANDA. What happened?…It's like a horrible dream.

ROGER. *(as the doctor)* I'm afraid while you were in the bathroom Henry died.

WANDA. Oh, no..

(She begins to cry hysterically. She grabs the towel that **JULES** *used to clean off his clown white and buries her face in it crying.)*

JULES. Yes, that's true…and that's why we can't accept your money.

ROGER. But Roger Gallais did find him.

JULES. Roger Gallais is not here, so I speak for the company.

ROGER. I'm sure Roger Gallais would not agree to this.

SHELLY. You don't even know Roger Gallais. How can you say what he'd agree to?

ROGER. I can't really but…we have the same accountant at Wells Fargo bank.

SHELLY. Why don't you go back to Iran or Cedar Sinai or where ever you came from! Can't you see she's upset! Don't people in L.A. have any human feelings? *(to* **WANDA** *who is still crying)* KNOCK IT OFF!

(She stops crying.)

JULES. And I'm sure Roger Gallais would agree with me, doctor! Here's your cheque.

*(***WANDA*** thinks for a long moment. A realization is sinking in.)*

WANDA. Maybe that man who died wasn't Henry. Maybe he didn't have amnesia. But what about true love?

SHELLY. True love only comes with batteries.

WANDA. What about Henry? Where can I find him?

JULES. I don't know where you're going to find him, but I do know you're not going to find him here.

SHELLY. Come on, I'll take you to the airport.

WANDA. Thanks…Jules, you know, you're really very kind.

(She kisses him lightly. She drops a handkerchief. They exit.)

JULES. You dropped your handkerchief…

(He looks at the handkerchief longingly.)

ROGER. Wonderful! Great, Jules! Now, what are we going to do? This building ceases to be ours by tomorrow morning.

JULES. We'll just have to get another location.

*(***HARVEY MARTIN***, a gay activist, appears at the window. He wears short pants and sun glasses on the top of his head. He is in his mid-thirties, short back and sides with mustache. He can be played by the same actor who plays* **NOBBY***. He sings Camelot.)*

HARVEY. *(singing)* Camelot! Camelot! From far off France I hear you call. Camelot! Camelot! For you alone I give my all.

ROGER. Jules, there is a man at the window singing Camelot…badly.

JULES. May I help you?

HARVEY. *(head through window)* You certainly may!! Hi, I'm Harvey Martin, the gay activist running for West Hollywood City council. Have you heard of me?

BOTH. No!

HARVEY. Well, you soon will! Remember tomorrow is Election Day! If we were in Japan, it would be erection day! *(laughs at his own joke)* May I come in and talk to you on some very important issues facing our community.

ROGER. At the moment, we're rather busy!

JULES. Thank you!

*(He shuts the window and **HARVEY** disappears.)*

ROGER. Now, Jules, we need $1500 by tomorrow morning! Where do we get it? Please explain.

*(**HARVEY** enters on roller blades.)*

HARVEY. I'd like to explain a little bit about myself. Harvey Martin supports the unfortunates, disabled, blind, homeless, and "celebrity shut-ins." –

JULES. What's that?

HARVEY. People too famous to be seen in public. If elected, I will continue to make our city, West Hollywood, safe for movie stars and a living model of "Camelot."

ROGER. Camelot?

HARVEY. Yes, I thought it was a cute slogan, don't you?

(He sings and skates.)

A law was made a distant moon ago. July and August cannot be too hot and there is a legal limit to snow in Camelot! Camelot!

(stops singing)

I'm also with the gay men's choir. Would you like to buy some tickets? Two for one on Thursday! Of course, no obligation.

ROGER. *(to* **JULES***)* He doesn't miss a trick.

HARVEY. I try not to. You are voting on Tuesday, aren't you?

ROGER. Look, Mary Poppins, I can't vote because we're being evicted tomorrow and this building is being torn down.

HARVEY. Are you kidding, honey? They can't tear this building down!

ROGER. Sure they can.

HARVEY. You haven't heard of the "Harvey Martin initiative?" It was in the paper this morning!

JULES. No, what is it?

HARVEY. My friend Peter and I, were just walking around West Hollywood looking at all the old wonderful building being torn down. And I said, " Peter, we just have to save them." So, last week, my initiative passed and there is a moratorium on pre-1940 structures.

ROGER. Yeah, this building was built in 1939. She can't tear it down.

HARVEY. There's only one small detail, mon cher. You have to register it with the City of West Hollywood.

JULES. How do we do that?

HARVEY. Easy, you take the original deed to City Hall.

ROGER. Can't the city find a copy for us?

HARVEY. Are you kidding? That gaggle of queens couldn't find a seven-foot transvestite on Gay Pride day, let alone a 1939 deed. Trust me, go down there yourself and see my friend Peter. He works in the records departments. Tell him Harvey sent you.

ROGER. Thanks a lot, Harvey.

HARVEY. Now, who are you voting for tomorrow?

BOTH. Harvey Martin!

HARVEY. See you later, fellas.

(He exits singing Camelot.)

ROGER. You heard what he said?

JULES. We've got to take the original deed down to city hall and register it.

ROGER. And the original deed is in the safe.

JULES. And the safe is behind the picture on the wall.

ROGER. Well, where's the key to the safe?

JULES. Remember, you told me, "Hide it in plain sight." It's hanging on the wall attached to the bathroom key.

(They both smile triumphantly as they turn to where the key is hanging. It's not there!)

ROGER. Where is it?…Where is the goddamn Key?

JULES. There! Where's the goddamn key. It's suppose to be there…Wait a minute!

ROGER. Let's not panic…It must be here somewhere!

JULES. I'll check the bathroom. *(He knocks on the door.)*

ROGER. Nobody's in there, you idiot.

(He exits/returns. **ROGER** *begins to shift papers around and look under things.)*

JULES. It's not there!

(A long moment and then they manically throw paper searching everywhere.)

ROGER. Wait! Who was the last one to go into the bathroom?

BOTH. WANDA!

JULES. She must have the key!

ROGER. Where did she go?

JULES. Oklahoma! Texas! Timbuktu! I don't know.

(They both scream.)

End of Act I

ACT II

(ROGER and JULES are in the same position and still screaming. It is now night.)

ROGER. I'll try everyone named Wanda in El Paso.

JULES. I'll try Dallas, Fort Worth, and Amarillo.

(SHELLY enters. ROGER and JULES rush to her.)

ROGER & JULES. Where'd you take her? What airline? Did she give you a number?

SHELLY. Guys! Guys! Slow down! Now, one at a time.

ROGER. We've gotta find Wanda!

SHELLY. But, you just sent her away. I saw you!

ROGER. Where did she go?

SHELLY. Home.

ROGER. Where's that?

SHELLY. How should I know?

JULES. We're desperate. She's got the key to the bathroom!

SHELLY. Why don't you go across the street to the gas station?

ROGER. The key to the safe was attached to the bathroom key.

SHELLY. You guys got some real problems. *(She laughs.)*

ROGER. *(imitating SHELLY)* You guys got some real problems!

SHELLY. There's no need to be bitter!

ROGER. You right. We've got to reason this out! I got it, we'll blow up the safe.

SHELLY. Then you might burn everything inside, you putz!

JULES. She's right, you putz!

ROGER. *(annoyed)* I KNOW SHE'S RIGHT!

SHELLY. Wait a minute, I got an idea…One of the bartenders at the Comedy Store says he knows people.

ROGER. I know people! He knows people! What's that suppose to mean?

SHELLY. I'll bet he'd know a safe cracker.

JULES. You really think so?

SHELLY. I am supposed to do my act at the Comedy Store tonight. He'd probably be there.

ROGER. What are we waiting for? Let's go!

SHELLY. Wait a minute. If I do this, you guys gotta promise me something.

BOTH. Sure! Of course.

SHELLY. I'm going on tonight at 1 a.m. It is a Monday so there probably won't be anyone else there but you! So you got to promise to stay for my act.

BOTH. Fine! Great! You got it!

(They go for the door.)

SHELLY. Hey! Hey! I'm not finished! You gotta laugh at the jokes even if you'd heard them before. And then, when my act is over, tell Mitzy, she's the owner of the club, that Shelly Levine is the funniest performer you've ever seen and that she should give her a regular spot. Is it a deal?

(They nod in agreement.)

I love you guys!

(They exit and turn off the lights)

*(A beat passes and **NOBBY** appears at the window. He has the same awkward struggle getting through the window as he did in Act I. **LOLA** again comes through the door and looks at him with a "haven't you learned yet" look. **NOBBY** and **LOLA** look around.)*

LOLA. Check the closets too. (**NOBBY** *picks up a donut.*) The donuts are for the customers!

*(**NOBBY** puts the donut back and goes into the room offstage.)*

NOBBY. *(whispering)* Okay! Great, no one about. We'll blow the place straight away.

LOLA. Wait, there is one small detail. We have to open the safe and get the deed to the building.

NOBBY. Why?

(LOLA turns on the light.)

LOLA. That's a fire proof safe. If the deed survives the fire that could prove a motive for Lola to burn the building down. Then, Lola and Nobby would not pass "GO" but go directly to jail and they wouldn't collect one million dollars. And, we wouldn't want that to happen, would we?

(LOLA removes a picture on the wall to expose the safe.
NOBBY *crosses and examines it.)*

NOBBY. No…Stone me! That's a bugger of a job. It'll take half the night.

LOLA. No, it won't because I know where the key is.

NOBBY. You do! Where?

LOLA. Those two pendejos think they're very smart. They will hide the key in plain sight. Do you see it? It's right in front of your eyes.

NOBBY. No, I don't see it. Where is it for Godsake?

LOLA. *(pointing)* Right there. Madre de Dios! No está! Where the hell is the bathroom key?

NOBBY. The door's open. You don't need it, love. I won't look. Ha ha….

LOLA. I don't want to go to the bathroom!

NOBBY. Then what do you want the bleeding key for?

LOLA. To open the safe!

NOBBY. You can't open the safe with a lavatory key.

LOLA. ¡Idiota! Ya lo sé! The key for the safe was on the same ring.

NOBBY. What a daft place to put a key.

LOLA. I didn't put it there! We have to now break the safe!

NOBBY. Christ, break into that! Well, I'd better go get me tools from the boot.

(He starts to go out the window.)

LOLA. Why don't you use the door?

NOBBY. Right.

(He exits by the door.)

LOLA. *(looking up to heaven)* Why, God, do things not go smoothly for Lola?

(WANDA enters. She carries a suitcase. LOLA sees her and gets an idea. She steps into the closet.)

WANDA. Hello, anyone here.

(LOLA enters from the closet carrying a dust mop and apron. She pretends to be a maid and speaks with a very heavy accent.)

Excuse me, but I was looking for Jules.

LOLA. Señor Mr. Jules he no here right now. What you want Señora?

WANDA. Oh, I have something of his I want to return.

LOLA. He no here, mi hija. You have come back…Un momento, what you have ?

WANDA. Oh, nothing important, just a key.

LOLA. La Llave! Why no give me and I give him!

WANDA. It's sort of personal and I want to give it to him myself.

LOLA. It no the bathroom key?

WANDA. Why? Yes it is.

LOLA. We've been looking for it everywhere. Give me, I open bathroom door. I have clean ring around toilet. Then I'll give back you.

(WANDA hesitates a moment and then gives it to LOLA.)

Ay gracias, Señora…

(LOLA takes it removing the smaller safe key as she exits. NOBBY enters with his "tools" a very large sledge hammer and crowbar.)

WANDA. Hi, I'm Wanda. I'm waiting for Jules. What are you doing with all those tools?

NOBBY. Ha-ha…err…

(**LOLA** *enters and sees the situation.*)

LOLA. Oh, that's Jose,….

NOBBY. Jose?

LOLA. He no speak English.

NOBBY. *(He speaks with heavy English accent.)* Yes, I mean er…si si, correcto, no hablo ingles. Estoy Mexicano.

WANDA. Oh, he's from Mexico, what part?

NOBBY.	**LOLA.**
Tijuana!	Mexico City.

LOLA. Mexico City via Tijuana.

WANDA. What's he doing with that big hammer?

NOBBY. Estoy carpintero.

WANDA. That's funny, my uncle was a carpenter and he never had a hammer that big.

(**LOLA** *takes* **WANDA** *by the arm and tries to lead her out.*)

LOLA. He's a Mexican carpenter. Señor Jules no here. Why no you come back tomorrow, querida?

(**WANDA** *breaks away.*)

WANDA. I think I'll just wait.

LOLA. Maybe a long time.

NOBBY. Si, mucho tiempo!

WANDA. Oh, I don't mind. I really don't have anywhere else to go.

(**LOLA** *and* **NOBBY** *stare at each other in frustration.*)

LOLA. We going home a few minutes and we locking office, señorita. You no can stay.

WANDA. Of course, I'll leave. *(She slaps her own wrist.)* Bad Wanda…bad girl.

(She walks out the door and stands by the window looking in.)

WANDA. *(cont.)* Oh, I guess, I'll wait outside until Jules comes. Do you have magazine…Never mind, I'll just count to myself…one, two, three, four.

LOLA. You going to wait outside and count to yourself? I feel bad for you but we have close. But, before, how you like a coffee and a donut?

WANDA. That sounds great!

NOBBY. Si, yo tambien. Me gusta los donutos.

LOLA. *(She glares at him.)* Quedate con la boca cerrada, por favor!

(She crosses to NOBBY and when WANDA isn't looking, knees him in the groin. She smiles broadly and then crosses to the coffee pot and pours coffee. She drops a small tablet in the cup.)

Cream and sugar?

WANDA. Sweet and low, if you have it. *(looking at NOBBY bent over)* What's wrong with him?

LOLA. He has Montezuma's Revenge!

WANDA. Don't you get that from drinking the water?

LOLA. Don't worry we've boiled the water for the coffee.

(LOLA hands her the coffee and a donut. WANDA hesitates.)

WANDA. Gracias, señora.

LOLA. *(annoyed)* I am a señorita. You speak a little Spanish, no?

WANDA. Yes, I had two years in high school. Me llamo es Wanda, ..wamma yamma…

LOLA. ¡Qué, bueno!

(LOLA grabs WANDA and forces her to drink the coffee.)

WANDA. *(She reacts to the drug.)* Gosh, I can hardly keep my eyes open.

LOLA. It's probably all that Spanish.

(A few moments pass and WANDA falls asleep.)

NOBBY. ¿Qué pasa, ahora?

LOLA. *(She speaks to him like a child.)* Take the key and open the safe.

NOBBY. I've never opened a safe with a key before...I can't be that hard.

(**NOBBY** *crosses to the wall safe. He places the key in the lock. He begins to twist the key. There seems to be a problem, he begins to shake it.*)

Oh, dear.

LOLA. What is it!

NOBBY. I just broke the key off in the lock!

LOLA. ¡Hijo de lo mas tonta que hay! ¿Ahora, que, vamos hacer?

NOBBY. What are you saying.

LOLA. Now what are we going to do?

NOBBY. I once blew up a pub in Bradford with dynamite.

LOLA. Do you have any dynamite?

NOBBY. No, but I know where I can get some!

(**WANDA** *stretches and moves.*)

Christ, she's going to wake up.

(Car door slams. **LOLA** *looks out the window.)*

LOLA. ¡Que mala Suerte! Somebody comes! We have to come back when they leave.

(**NOBBY** *moves toward the door.*)

The Window! The Window!

(They exit out the window.)

(**JULES** *enters. He has a sad look. He holds* **WANDA**'s *handkerchief.*)

JULES. Wanda...Wanda.

(**WANDA** *wakes with a start.*)

WANDA. Oh, there you are.

JULES. WANDA!

WANDA. Hi, I must have fallen asleep.

JULES. Wanda, what are you doing here? Why did you come back?

WANDA. Well, why do you think, silly?

JULES. Not to see me?

WANDA. Of course, who else?

JULES. I never thought I'd see you again.

WANDA. How did it make you feel?

JULES. Not real good.

WANDA. I never thought I'd see you again, Jules.

JULES. And, how did it make you feel?

WANDA. Not real good.

JULES. I don't have anything to offer you.

WANDA. Yes, you do, Jules. You're very sweet and very kind and you stopped me from being cheated.

JULES. Well, that was easy because I was the one doing the cheating.

WANDA. You probably should have. It would've taught me a lesson.

JULES. No, that's not me or not Roger either, but a situation can make people do things they really don't want to do.

WANDA. Like a lonely woman trying to recapture some silly college romance. It was a crazy and immature idea. Even if I'd found him, I wasn't really going to marry him.

JULES. I'm glad about that.

WANDA. You are?

JULES. Yeah…

WANDA. Well, then, I'm glad about that. Jules, may I kiss you?

JULES. Sure.

(They kiss. A beat. They break apart at the sound of a noise. **ROGER** *enters.)*

ROGER. *(seeing* **WANDA***)* Boy, am I glad to see you!

WANDA. Hi, Roger, I decided not to go back to Texas just yet.

ROGER. You just don't happen to have the bathroom key do you?

WANDA. Yes, I do.

(She produces the keys and hand them to him. He grabs them but quickly notices the safe key is missing.)

ROGER. Where's the little key?

WANDA. It was there. I'll bet that woman took it.

ROGER. What woman?

WANDA. It's all kind of vague, like a dream. They were here and I don't know…but it seemed like she had something to hide. Then I fell asleep.

ROGER. Lola! Who was with her?

WANDA. José.

ROGER\ JULES. José?

WANDA. She said he spoke only Spanish but he had the weirdest accent I ever heard.

JULES. Did he sound like this: (**JULES** *imitates* **NOBBY**) "Buenos trades Señores y Señoras!"?

WANDA. Yes!

BOTH. Nobby!

WANDA. I had a feeling they were up to something.

JULES. Why?

WANDA. By the way they were talking, it seemed they were making some kind of plan.

ROGER. What did they say?

WANDA. I don't know, I was half asleep. I felt like I was drugged.

*(**ROGER** notices the coffee cup. He picks it up and smells it.)*

ROGER. You were. I wish we could find out what they were planning.

JULES. There's a way we could find out.

WANDA & ROGER. How?

JULES. It's a long shot and it involves some big risks for Wanda.

ROGER. Fine, I don't care about that!...I mean, what risks? We wouldn't want anything bad to happen to Wanda.

WANDA. What could happen?

JULES. Let me explain my theory first. I believe, Wanda's unconscious mind recorded what happened. So, what we have to do is release your unconscious mind.

WANDA. How can we do that?

JULES. I think I can program the transcabator to do that. But if I'm wrong, it could cleanse your brain.

WANDA. What effect would it have?

JULES. We can't do it!

ROGER. Why! Why not?

JULES. It's very technical but we need three people to operate the transcabator and there is only Roger and I.

*(The door is thrown open and **SHELLY** enters.)*

SHELLY. Boy, am I pissed at you guys! I thought you were my friends! Friends in California, ha! Why did you guys walk out on my act?

ROGER. We thought it was over.

JULES. They turned out the lights.

SHELLY. Mitzy told them to turn out the lights.

JULES. Why?

SHELLY. *(trying to hold back tears)* Oh, I don't know...the Comedy Store's a dump... I'm not working there any more..... I'm no good...Who am I kidding?...Shelly Levine stand-up comic...Ha... Mitzy told me not to come back.

*(**ROGER** and **JULES** embrace her.)*

ROGER. What's she know? ...I liked it...I thought you were real funny.

JULES. Me too...everyone in the audience though you were terrific.

WANDA. I'll see your show next time!

SHELLY. You liked me?...You really like me?

*(**ROGER** begins to massage her shoulders.)*

ROGER. Do you think you could do us a favor?

SHELLY. What is it?

ROGER. We have to open up Wanda's mind...

JULES. And we were wondering if you could help us.

SHELLY. Oh no, that's too weird. Only in California do you find Kookoids like you guys!

ROGER. Kookoids who believe in you! You could be the new Howard Stern. *(Note: Actor can use current name.)*

SHELLY. I could be crass and disgusting and make a million bucks a year.

JULES. You're already crass and disgusting

SHELLY. I know I am....Okay, what do you want me to do?

JULES. Get the transcabator ready. I'll get Wanda ready.

*(**WANDA** sits in the Transcabator chair while business to be arranged.)*

Now, let me explain, we are involved in a four step process. One, we must neutralize the mind. Two, we induce a mega thought. Three, the Transcabator turns the mind into a computer. Four, the extraction process. And, five the data is transferred into the Transcabator. Now, Wanda's data will be processed into my mind, but one mistake and...Push the button.

*(**JULES** puts on head gear similar to **WANDA**'s. **SHELLY** and **ROGER** man their places as **JULES** turns on the transcabator. The lights dim and a special goes on **WANDA**, which will give the effect of turning her different colors. Finally she is bathed in a pure white light.)*

Her mind is neutralized. Station one, stand by.

SHELLY. Roger.

ROGER. What?

SHELLY. Station one, standing by.

JULES. Induce mega-thought!

SHELLY. Roger!

ROGER. What is it?

SHELLY. *(pulling switches)* I don't mean you Roger and Jules, I mean Roger...Get it?

ROGER. Yeah, I think so.

SHELLY. Mega-thought induced.

(SFX: loud noise.)

JULES. Activate transcabator.

SHELLY. Roger.

ROGER. Jules!

JULES. What?

ROGER. Nothing! Transcabator activated!

(At this point lots of noise, flashing lights. **JULES** *and* **WANDA** *begin talking like tape recorder on fast-forward.)*

SHELLY. What are they doing?

ROGER. Transferring data!

(They continue to make noise for a few more beats.)

SHELLY. Red Alert. Mind erase function operative. Erase 2008. –6-5-4-3-2-1.

ROGER. Erase the 1980s. Erase the 1970s.

(ROGER *begins to hit a series of computer command buttons.)*

SHELLY. ...1969...1969...What have you done?

ROGER. I have just entered a temporary pause break in his brain. It's August 16, 1969.

*(***JULES** *and* **WANDA** *are now 60s hippies smoking pot.)*

JULES. Hey, man don't bogart that joint.

WANDA. Make love, not war...

JULES. Heavy, man, there's Ravi Shankar, man...

ROGER. Now, I want you to scroll back and interface his mind with the over drive hard disk.

*(***SHELLY** *begins to do a series of computer commands.)*

SHELLY. 1970s...restored, 1980s restored. 1990s restored. Brain restoration completed.

(The transcabator shuts itself off. **SHELLY** *and* **ROGER** *remove the head sets off* **WANDA** *and* **JULES**. **WANDA** *rushes to* **JULES** *who is still a bit groggy.)*

WANDA. Are you alright, my darling?

JULES. Yeah, I think so, but I felt like I was at Woodstock.

ROGER. Well? What happened?

JULES. It rained the whole time! Bummer.

SHELLY. Did you filter the information?

JULES. *(He closes his eyes.)* House key…explosion time, I need help. Help me Wanda, help me get you out of my mind!

(They press their heads together and close their eyes. **JULES'** *head goes behind* **WANDA**. *He speaks, she moves her lips.)*

WANDA\JULES. They're going to remove the deed from the safe…and then blow up the house.

ROGER. So, they've got the key alright.

WANDA. We'd better call the police!

ROGER. No, no, don't call the police. I have too many parking tickets!

SHELLY. When are they coming?

*(***JULES'*** put his head behind* **WANDA** *and speaks.)*

WANDA\JULES. Pretty soon.

WANDA. Jules, I was so worried about you.

JULES. You risked your life for me, it was the least I could do.

WANDA. I have this funny feeling about you, Jules.

JULES. And, I have a funny feeling about you, Wanda.

ROGER. It's love. I had it once with Lola.

WANDA. What happened between you two?

ROGER. I'm not really sure. Somehow things just went wrong. Sometimes I miss her a lot. Hey, they're going to be here pretty soon. You guys get out of here.

WANDA. What are you going to do?

ROGER. I just got an idea how I'm going to win this game. Go on, get out of here!

(They all leave and **ROGER** *turns off the lights and hides in the next room. A beat passes and* **NOBBY** *appears at the window and climbs in clumsily.* **LOLA** *enters by the door. They are dressed in overcoats and burglar-type gear.)*

LOLA. Will you stop coming through the pinche window!

NOBBY. Sorry love, old habits are hard to break.

*(***NOBBY*** has a kit bag from which he removes a small bundle of red stick dynamite. As he talks, he crudely tapes two stick of dynamite to the safe.* **LOLA** *looks at him with disbelief.)*

LOLA. What about the noise? The neighbors?

NOBBY. Don't worry about it.

LOLA. Oh sorry, is this the new silent dynamite?

NOBBY. It'll be so quick no one will notice. Brill, isn't it?

LOLA. Santa Madre, maybe Roger wasn't such a bad guy after all. For sure, he wasn't as stupid as you.

NOBBY. Leave it out, love.

*(***NOBBY*** lights a match and is about to light the dynamite fuse when the lights are thrown on full. Both he and* **LOLA** *give a start.* **ROGER** *steps into the room.)*

ROGER. I thought you didn't take over till tomorrow morning.

LOLA. I'm just inspecting my property.

ROGER. Sounds like you don't trust me!

LOLA. I don't.

*(***NOBBY*** burns himself and yells.)*

ROGER. You're gonna blow the safe? Lola, I didn't think you were so dumb!

LOLA. Dumb! I'm going to get a million dollars!

ROGER. You are going to get eight years. How stupid do you think the cops are? And speaking of dumb! *(He looks at* **NOBBY**.*)* Lola, I want to talk to you alone.

LOLA. Beat it, Nobby.

(**NOBBY** *exits.*)

ROGER. Lola, I'm going to stop you from doing this.

LOLA. How?

ROGER. Easy, I'm not going to fight you. You can have the house. You can have a divorce.

LOLA. Wait a minute! After all this fighting, why are you giving up?

ROGER. Why? You could say for old time's sake...sentimentality. Maybe, I'm paying off my debt to nostalgia.

LOLA. Are you turning soft on me, Roger?

ROGER. Maybe...I was just thinking about a smoky club south of the border and a girl named Lola.

(FLASH BACK)

(The lights change and Perez Prado's "Cherry Pink and Apple Blossom White" (or some type of Latin music) plays. The set should transform as much as possible to a read hot "South of the Border," Latin night club. **LOLA** *removes her coat. She wears a sexy red dress with a split up the side. The actors, other than* **LOLA** *and* **ROGER** *are now playing other people.* **ROGER** *removes his coat and is dressed in a whilte sailor uniform.* **LOLA** *moves about singing BESAME MUCHO. She pays more than a little attention to the handsome young sailor.)*

LOLA. Besame, Besame mucho, cuando tus lapios me acercan la ultima vez....etc.

*(**LOLA** and **ROGER** are much younger and the scene is more like two teenager in first love.)*

ROGER. Err...Don't I know you from some where?

LOLA. Is that the best you can do, Gringo?

ROGER. At the moment...Hey, what's your name?

LOLA. Lola...Lola Montezuma.

ROGER. Montezuma! Isn't that the name of a delicious beer they sell at the colorful club in Tijuana?

LOLA. What's your name?

ROGER. Roger...Roger Gallais.

LOLA. Roger Gallais, isn't that the name of a perfume they sell at those trendy boutiques on Hollywood and Vine?

ROGER. Why don't we get out of here?

LOLA. I can't...

ROGER. Why not?

LOLA. Because of...HIM!

(Fast mambo music is heard. The actor who plays **JULES** *enters wearing a zoot suit. He is now Manolo – "El Gran Mambero." He mambos.)*

ROGER. Who's he?

LOLA. Manolo! He won me in a mambo contest! I'm his until.... *(She begins to cry.)*

ROGER. Until what?

LOLA. Until someone can...out mambo Manolo.

(She looks at him longingly.)

ROGER. I'll do it...Teach me how to mambo.

LOLA. Are you crazy, gringo! No one has ever beaten Manolo!

ROGER. It's our only chance for happiness.

LOLA. Can you do this.

(She does a few steps. He follows. She does a few more. He follows.)

MANOLO. What are you doing, Lola?

LOLA. I want to leave with the gringo.

MANOLO. You know the rules.

ROGER. And so do I, Manolo! I challenge you to Mambo!

MANOLO. You, a mere gringo, challenge me Manolo, The greatest Mambero in all of Tijuana...to Mambo?

(Everyone laughs.)

Alright, Gringo I take your challenge. *We mambo for Lola!!!*

*(****MANOLO*** *grabs one of the girls and mambos a few steps. He does the same with another. Then points at*

LOLA. *They mambo. He stops and holds up his hands a like a triumphant Bull Fighter, everyone cheers.)*

*(***ROGER** *mambos like Gene Kelly. This can be a big production number. He grabs a girl, then he grabs* **LOLA,** *they mambo.)*

LOLA. I choose the Gringo.

(blackout)

(The actors put their coats back on and they have returned to the present.)

ROGER. Sometimes all that seems like a long time ago

LOLA. And sometimes it seems like yesterday.

ROGER.	**LOLA.**
Why did we ever…	What did we ever…

(They both stop themselves from going on. They stare and then return to the present situation.)

*(***ROGER** *crosses to the safe and examines it. He picks up a screwdriver from* **NOBBY***'s kit.)*

ROGER. You broke the key off. *(He opens the safe.)*

LOLA. That was Nobby.

ROGER. Here's the deed and here's the divorce papers. It's all yours, just let me pick up my things in the morning.

LOLA. Sure.

ROGER. So long, Lola.

(He starts to leave.)

LOLA. Hey, wait a minute. Aren't you going to kiss me goodbye?

ROGER. Sure.

*(***ROGER** *blows her a kiss. She grabs it out of the air passionately and rubs it on her body.)*

LOLA. Don't forget me.

ROGER. Don't worry, I won't.

*(***ROGER** *exits as* **NOBBY** *enters.)*

NOBBY. Stone me! After all we've gone through, he's chucking in the towel. What a wanker!

LOLA. Shut up, will you, Nobby? Let's get out of here.

NOBBY. Right.

(**NOBBY** *crosses to the heater and opens it.*)

LOLA. What are you doing?

NOBBY. We're still goin' to blow the place, in't we?

LOLA. I promised him he could pick up his stuff tomorrow!

NOBBY. He can. It'll just be a bit more spread out! Ha, ha, ha.

(*He goes back to working on the heater.*)

LOLA. I said, no!

NOBBY. If the city finds out or he tells them, we've had it. They'll stop us. No mini mall! No million bucks!

LOLA. I said, NO!

(**NOBBY** *is quite angry. They just stare at each other for a long moment.*)

NOBBY. Alright, Lola, you're the Governor this time. But when I'm your husband, I warn you, things will be different.

LOLA. I don't think you are ever going to be my husband, Nobby. Let's go!

NOBBY. What do you mean by that, you tortilla eating cow!

LOLA. We're finished, Nobby, finito, terminado…The party's over. It's cheerio.

NOBBY. You still fancy Roger, don't you.

LOLA. I don't know. But I don't fancy you!

NOBBY. After all this, you think you're going to cut me out of a million bucks. You must be joking, love.

LOLA. I'm not joking, Nobby.

NOBBY. You're not? Then, I've got a surprise for you.

(*He grabs her and twists her arm behind her back and forces her into a chair. From his kit bag, he removes a rope and ties her in the chair.*)

LOLA. Just what do you think you're doing?

NOBBY. It's quite simple, we're partners on this deal, if one of us was "accidentally killed" the other gets one hundred percent of the moola. It's in the contract!

LOLA. You'll never get away with it!

NOBBY. Won't I?

LOLA. How will you explain it to the cops?

NOBBY. I was tired and left you here by yourself. I went straight home to bed. There was a faulty switch on the heater. The house filled with gas. You fell unconscious. Then the place blew up. Terrible shame. I shall buy a nice proper wreath for your funeral.

LOLA. ¡Hijo de la Gran Chingada!

NOBBY. Bye, Lola, it's been swell.

*(He moves towards the door. Suddenly **ROGER** comes in.)*

ROGER. Sorry, I just thought I'd get some of…Hey, why are you tied? What's going on here?

NOBBY. *(with his gun out)* We were having a little farewell party and you're invited. Sit in that chair.

*(**ROGER** throws his coat at **NOBBY** and misses. He puts his hands up and sits in the chair. **NOBBY** ties **ROGER** in the chair with the belt from his overcoat.)*

ROGER. You won't get away with this, Nobby.

NOBBY. Won't I?

ROGER. How will you explain it to the cops?

NOBBY. I was tired and left you and Lola here by yourselves. I went straight home to bed. There was a faulty switch on the heater. The house filled with gas. Both of you fell unconscious and then the place blew up. Terrible shame. I shall buy a nice proper wreath for your funerals.

*(There is a noise off. **NOBBY** flattens himself against the wall and draws his pistol. The door is flung open and **JULES** and **WANDA** enter. The gun is knocked from **NOBBY**'s hand. **WANDA** picks it up.)*

WANDA. You dropped this.

*(She hands **NOBBY** the gun.)*

JULES. Roger, why are you tied up?

WANDA. Why is your housekeeper tied up?

NOBBY. We're having a little farewell party. You're invited. Get that chair! Put it there! Now sit in it!

*(**WANDA** and **JULES** sit in the chair.)*

JULES. You won't get away with this!

NOBBY. Won't I?

*(**NOBBY** begins to tie them up with **JULES**' suspenders.)*

WANDA. How will you explain it to the police?

NOBBY. Er…Well, I was tired and I, er, left you and Lola and Roger and him here….You were playing a game of musical chairs. Then I went straight home to bed. There was a faulty switch on the heater. The house filled with gas…

ROGER. And I suppose none of us smelled the gas?

LOLA. We were too involved playing musical chairs?

NOBBY. That's right!

ROGER. And then, we tied ourselves up because it was a sado masochistic game of musical chairs?

NOBBY. Good idea! You Yanks are a kinky lot! Anyway, all of you fell unconscious and then the house blew up. Quite simple, really. I shall buy a nice proper wreath for your funerals…

*(**SHELLY** enters.)*

SHELLY. Hey, were you guys playing a game of sado masochistic musical chairs without me!

NOBBY. Would you like to play?

SHELLY. Sure…I brought my own cuffs!

*(She produces a pair of hand cuff and cuffs herself to **ROGER**.)*

Why does the gas man from outer space have a gun?

NOBBY. We're having a little farewell party and you're invited.

SHELLY. How're going to explain it to the cops?

NOBBY. I was tired and…

ALL. Oh, shut up!

NOBBY. You've got two minutes to say your prayers. That is more or less two minutes, perhaps three, even four. I'm not really sure. Anyway, Adios Amigos. And don't try to untie yourselves or I'll be back.

*(**NOBBY** grabs the box of donuts.)*

WANDA. Those are for the customers!

*(He bites into the donut. He doesn't like the taste. **NOBBY** exits.)*

ROGER. There's a letter opener in the desk.

LOLA. There's a cigarette lighter in my purse.

SHELLY. Good idea if you want to blow us up right now!

JULES. I think, you should try and bite through my suspenders!

WANDA. Not with this expensive dental work! Jules, our time together was very short…

JULES. But meaningful!

ROGER. I don't know how to say this Lola, but I wish things had been different.

LOLA. Me too…Roger, I lo…

(They begin to move around in the chairs trying to untie each other. During this scene, it is getting light outside.)

SHELLY. Hold your breath. Like you're under water.

(They all try to hold their breath but they slowly lose the battle and each one of them faints from the gas. A beat passes as they all are unconscious in their chairs.)

HARVEY. *(off stage singing)* Camelot! Camelot! From far off France I hear your call.

*(The door is thrown open and in marches **HARVEY MARTIN**. He smells the gas and turns it off and opens the window.)*

HARVEY. *(cont.)* My God, gas! This is dangerous. If you're dead you can't vote for me! Let's get some ventilation! Where are those Santa Ana winds when you need them?

(He starts reviving them.)

It's six o'clock in the morning! The polls have just opened. Everyone who's alive has to vote! Let me amend that, everyone who's alive has to vote for me.

(The group starts to come around. He begins to untie them.)

What was this, a game of "Sado Masochistic Musical Chairs"? I played it at my last birthday! Trust me, it always ends in tears.

*(He starts to give **ROGER** mouth to mouth restoration. **ROGER** wakes up.)*

(Everyone is untied.)

ROGER. I'm okay! Thanks, Harvey. I'd tell you what happened here but you wouldn't believe it!

HARVEY. This is West Hollywood, I'd believe it! Do you believe the Sheriff's department just arrested an English arsonist in front of your house.

ROGER. Everybody, this is Harvey Martin…

WANDA. Henry!

HARVEY. Wanda!

WANDA. I don't believe it! Is that really you?

HARVEY. Wanda!…Wanda Harrington! What are you doing in Los Angeles?

WANDA. I came to find you…Henry!

HARVEY. It's Harvey. Now…things have changed a little with me since High School.

WANDA. I can see that…But what about true love?

HARVEY. Oh, that, I think I found it.

WANDA. And so did I. *(She looks at **JULES**.)*

HARVEY. Congratulations. You must come to dinner and meet Peter. He's divine!

JULES. We'd love to meet your Peter…After the wedding.
ROGER. Wedding! Congratulations, I'm so happy for you.

(**ROGER**, *on the verge of tears, turns away.* **LOLA** *looks at him lovingly. They move toward each other and embrace.*)

LOLA. Roger, we almost spent our last moments on earth together.
ROGER. Yeah, I know…How would you like to spend the rest of our lives, together?

(They kiss.)

WANDA. Look, they've found it…true love.

(The birds tweet.)

SHELLY. I can't believe this…
HARVEY. What's the matter with you?
SHELLY. Oh, nothing except, I'm unfunny, unhappy and unmarried.
HARVEY. You must be from New York…You're Shelly Levine, I saw your act at the comedy store!
SHELLY. You did?
HARVEY. Yes, lights up a few jokes and lights out. Quick and to the point. I like that! Hey, how would you like to work on my acceptance speech?
SHELLY. Working in politics! At last a real comedy job!
HARVEY. That's right. Now, remember everyone,

(SONG)

A law was made a distant moon ago here.
(Add **SHELLY***)*
July and August cannot be too hot
(Add **JULES** *and* **WANDA***)*
So come here if you would, it's really awfully good
(Add **ROGER** *and* **LOLA***)*
For happily ever aftering here in West Hollywood.

The End

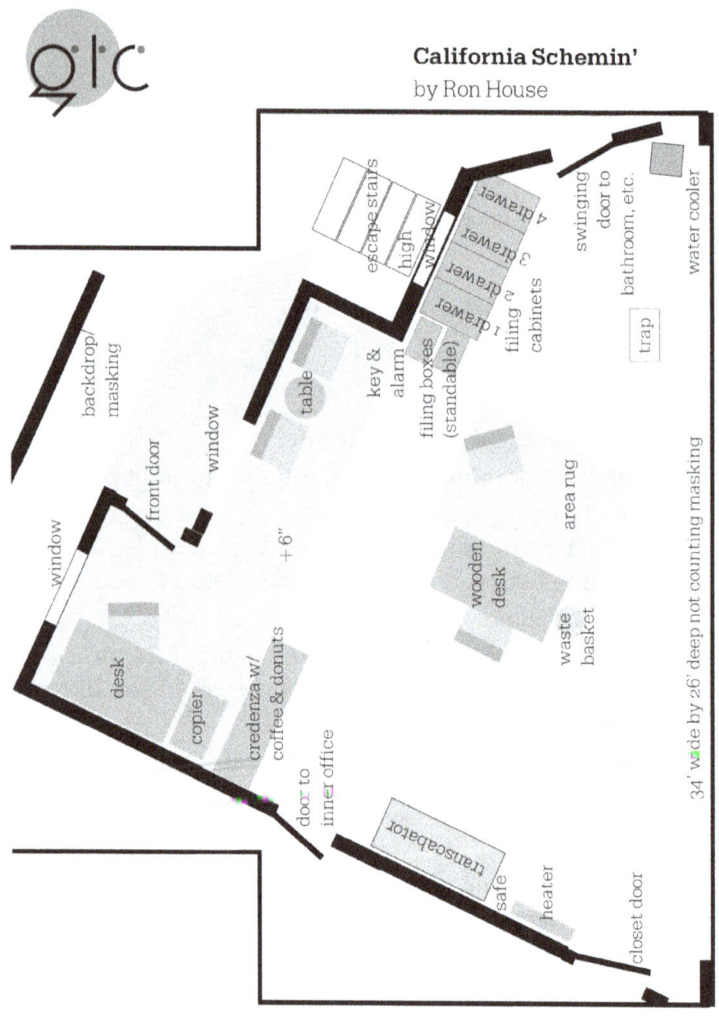

California Schemin'
by Ron House

design by Kevin Cochran
for Grove Theater Center

Co-authored by
Ron House...

El Grande de Coca Cola
Bullshot Crummond
Footlight Frenzy
The Scandalous Adventures of Sir Toby Trollope

Please visit our website **samuelfrench.com** for complete descriptions and licensing information.

www.ingramcontent.com/pod-product-compliance
Lightning Source LLC
Chambersburg PA
CBHW070649300426
44111CB00013B/2345